To

_____

From

_____

365 DAY BRIGHTENERS™

Whispered Words
OF ENCOURAGEMENT

365 Day Brighteners™ *Whispered Words of Encouragement*

Copyright © 2006 DaySpring® Cards.
Published by DaySpring® Cards, Inc.
Siloam Springs, Arkansas 72761
www.dayspring.com
Photo © Ryan McVey/Getty Images

Design by Franke Design, Minneapolis, Minnesota.

Except for Scripture verses, references to men and masculine
pronouns have been replaced with "people," "women," and gender-
neutral or feminine pronouns to personalize the quotes for you.

Scripture quotations are from the following sources: The HOLY BIBLE,
NEW INTERNATIONAL VERSION® (NIV®) © 1973, 1978, 1984 by International
Bible Society. Used by permission of Zondervan. THE MESSAGE © Eugene
H. Peterson 1993, 1994, 1995. Used by permission of NavPress Publishing
Group. All rights reserved. The Living Bible (TLB) © 1971 by permission of
Tyndale House Publishers, Inc., Wheaton, IL. The New Revised Standard
Version of the Bible (NRSV) © 1989 Division of Christian Education, National
Council of Churches. Used by permission of Zondervan. The New King
James Version (NKJV®), copyright 1979, 1980, 1982, Thomas Nelson, Inc.,
Publishers. J. B. Phillips: The New Testament in Modern English,
Revised Edition (PHILLIPS). Copyright © J. B. Phillips 1958, 1960, 1972.
Used by permission of Macmillan Publishing Co., Inc. All rights reserved.

ISBN 1594494940
Made in China

365 DAY BRIGHTENERS™

Whispered Words
OF ENCOURAGEMENT

Faith isn't the ability to believe
long and far into the misty future.
It's simply taking God at His
word and taking the next step.

JONI EARECKSON TADA

God loves to look at us, and loves it when we will look back at Him. Even when we try to run away from our troubles…God will find us, bless us, even when we feel most alone, unsure…. God will find a way to let us know that He is with us in this place, wherever we are.

KATHLEEN NORRIS

The Lord is...full of kindness.
He is close to all who call on Him
sincerely.... He hears their cries
for help and rescues them.
He protects all those who love Him.

PSALM 145:17-20 TLB

JANUARY 3

This new day brings
Another year,
Renewing hope...
Dispelling care.
And may we find
Before the end,
A deep content...
Another friend.

ARCH WARD

JANUARY 4

"Hope" is the thing with feathers—
That perches in the soul—
And sings the tune without
the words—
And never stops—at all.

EMILY DICKINSON

JANUARY 5

When we call on God,
He bends down His ear to listen,
as a father bends down
to listen to his little child.

ELIZABETH CHARLES

Everyone has inside himself
a piece of good news!
The good news is that you
really don't know how great
you can be, how much
you can love, what you
can accomplish and what
your potential is.

ANNE FRANK

JANUARY 7

Now to Him who is able to do
far more abundantly beyond all
that we ask or think, according to
the power that works within us,
to Him be the glory in the church
and in Christ Jesus to all generations
forever and ever. Amen.

EPHESIANS 3:20-21 NASB

Just don't give up trying to
do what you really want to do.
Where there is love and inspiration,
I don't think you can go wrong.

God says to His children:
Are you lonesome? Breathe out
My name. Come to Me and I
will be your friend. Are you sick?
Come to Me for healing.
Are you left out of things?
Feeling rejected and pushed aside?
Come home to Me.

ALICE CHAPIN

One kind word can warm
three winter months.

JAPANESE PROVERB

*Encourage one another
day after day.*

HEBREWS 3:13 NASB

JANUARY 11

When you're with someone
you trust in,
never needing to pretend,
Someone who helps you
know yourself...
you know you're with a friend.

AMANDA BRADLEY

You are my hiding place;
You will protect me from
trouble and surround me
with songs of deliverance.

PSALM 32:7 NIV

JANUARY 13

The truly happy people are those who have a source of happiness too deep to be seriously disturbed by ordinary troubles.

MARION K. RICH

JANUARY 14

Are you bored with life?
Then throw yourself into some
work you believe in with
all your heart; live for it,
die for it, and you will find
happiness that you had
thought could never be yours.

DALE CARNEGIE

If you want to be successful,
know what you are doing,
love what you are doing, and
believe in what you are doing.

WILL ROGERS

Hope does not necessarily
take the form of excessive
confidence; rather, it involves
the simple willingness
to take the next step.

STANLEY HAUERWAS

Give thanks in all circumstances,
for this is God's will for you
in Christ Jesus.

1 THESSALONIANS 5:18 NIV

JANUARY 18

Allow your dreams a place in your prayers and plans. God-given dreams can help you move into the future He is preparing for you.

BARBARA JOHNSON

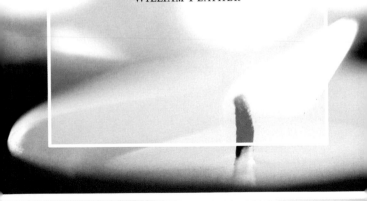

Success seems to be largely
a matter of hanging on
after others have let go.

WILLIAM FEATHER

JANUARY 20

To believe in God starts with
a conclusion about Him,
develops into confidence
in Him, and then matures
into a conversation with Him.

STUART BRISCOE

Always be in a state of
expectancy, and see that
you leave room for God
to come in as He likes.

OSWALD CHAMBERS

Come to Me, all who are weary
and heavy-laden, and I will give
you rest. Take My yoke upon you
and learn from Me, for I am
gentle and humble in heart,
and you will find rest for your souls.

MATTHEW 11:28-29 NASB

JANUARY 23

There is in every woman's heart
a spark of heavenly fire which
lies dormant in the broad daylight
of prosperity, but which kindles
up and beams and blazes
in the dark hour of adversity.

WASHINGTON IRVING

Never be afraid to trust
an unknown future
to an all-knowing God.

CORRIE TEN BOOM

*Cast your cares on the Lord
and He will sustain you.*

PSALM 55:22 NIV

JANUARY 25

The place where God calls
you to is the place where
your deep gladness and the
world's deep hunger meet.

FREDERICK BUECHNER

Genuine self-acceptance
is not derived from the power
of positive thinking, mind
games, or pop psychology.
It is an act of faith in the
grace of God alone.

BRENNAN MANNING

JANUARY 27

The Lord is close to
the brokenhearted
and saves those who
are crushed in spirit.

PSALM 34:18 NIV

Live for something....
Write your name in kindness,
love, and mercy on the
hearts of thousands you
come in contact with....
You will never be forgotten.

THOMAS CHALMERS

Everyday
Less like tearing more like building
Less like captive more like willing
Less like breakdown more
like surrender
Less like haunting more like remember
And I feel You here
You're picking up the pieces
Forever faithful.

SARA GROVES

God has a wonderful plan
for each person.... He knew
even before He created
this world what beauty He
would bring forth from our lives.

LOUIS B. WYLY

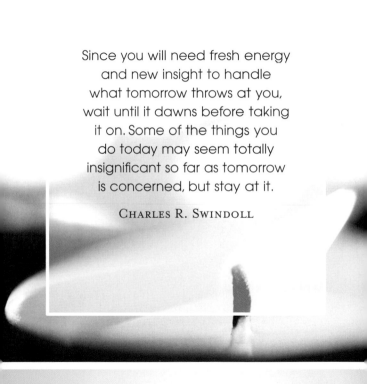

Since you will need fresh energy
and new insight to handle
what tomorrow throws at you,
wait until it dawns before taking
it on. Some of the things you
do today may seem totally
insignificant so far as tomorrow
is concerned, but stay at it.

CHARLES R. SWINDOLL

The steadfast love of the
Lord never ceases, His mercies
never come to an end;
they are new every morning;
great is Your faithfulness.

LAMENTATIONS 3:22-23 NRSV

FEBRUARY 2

All the beautiful sentiments
in the world weigh less
than a simple lovely action.

JAMES RUSSELL LOWELL

FEBRUARY 3

Caring words, friendship,
affectionate touch—all of these
have a healing quality. Why?
Because we were all created
by God to give and receive love.

JACK FROST

It is an awesome, challenging
thought: The Lord comes
to us in our friends. What we do
and are to them is an expression
of what we are to Him.

LLOYD JOHN OGILVIE

Faith goes up the stairs
that love has made
and looks out of the windows
which hope has opened.

CHARLES H. SPURGEON

Prayer is the key of the
morning and the bolt
on the door at night.

*I will trust and not be afraid,
for the Lord is my
strength and my song.*

Isaiah 12:2 TLB

Let your faith be in the quiet
confidence that God will every
day and every moment keep
you as the apple of His eye.

ANDREW MURRAY

FEBRUARY 8

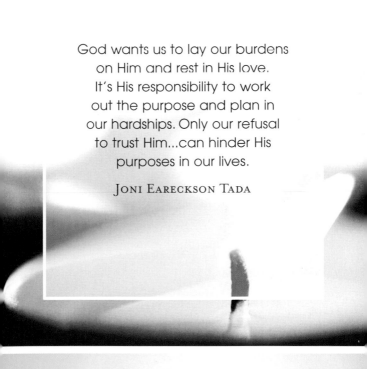

God wants us to lay our burdens
on Him and rest in His love.
It's His responsibility to work
out the purpose and plan in
our hardships. Only our refusal
to trust Him...can hinder His
purposes in our lives.

Joni Eareckson Tada

I know not where His islands lift
Their fronded palms in air;
I only know I cannot drift
Beyond His love and care.

JOHN GREENLEAF WHITTIER

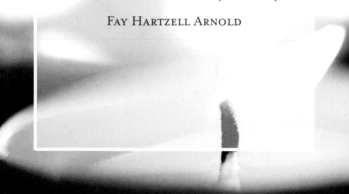

See each morning a world made
anew, as if it were the morning
of the very first day...
treasure and use it, as if it were
the final hour of the very last day.

FAY HARTZELL ARNOLD

May your roots go down deep
into the soil of God's marvelous love;
and may you be able to feel and
understand...how long, how wide,
how deep, and how high His love
really is; and to experience this love
for yourselves, though it is so great
that you will never see the end of it.

EPHESIANS 3:17-19 TLB

FEBRUARY 12

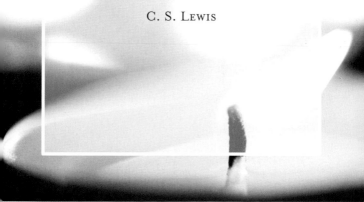

God loves us; not because we
are lovable but because He is love,
not because He needs to receive
but because He delights to give.

C. S. Lewis

February 13

There is a time for risky love.
There is a time for extravagant
gestures. There is a time to
pour out your affections on
one you love. And when the
time comes—seize it, don't miss it.

MAX LUCADO

Knowing what to say is not
always necessary; just the
presence of a caring friend can
make a world of difference.

SHERI CURRY

FEBRUARY 15

More and more I realize that
everybody, regardless of age,
needs to be hugged and comforted
in a brotherly or sisterly way
now and then. Preferably now.

JANE HOWARD

FEBRUARY 16

The Creator thinks enough of you
to have sent Someone very
special so that you might
have life—abundantly, joyfully,
completely, and victoriously.

*I have come that they may
have life, and that they may
have it more abundantly.*

JOHN 10:10 NKJV

FEBRUARY 17

We learn to believe by believing.
We learn to love by loving.
The practice of acting on a
certain thing, even (or especially)
when feeling is absent, embodies
the entire "how" of growth.

EUGENIA PRICE

FEBRUARY 18

When you are in the dark, listen,
and God will give you a very
precious message for someone
else when you get into the light.

Oswald Chambers

God washes the eyes by
tears until they can behold
the invisible land where
tears shall come no more.

HENRY WARD BEECHER

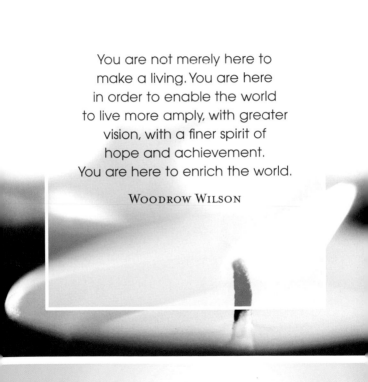

You are not merely here to
make a living. You are here
in order to enable the world
to live more amply, with greater
vision, with a finer spirit of
hope and achievement.
You are here to enrich the world.

WOODROW WILSON

FEBRUARY 21

He surrounds me with
loving-kindness and
tender mercies. He fills
my life with good things!

PSALM 103:4-5 TLB

FEBRUARY 22

The fullness of our heart
is expressed in our eyes,
in our touch, in what we
write, in what we say, in the
way we walk, the way we
receive, the way we need.

MOTHER TERESA

Remember that you are needed.
There is at least one important
work to be done that will
not be done unless you do it.

Charles Allen

February 24

If we celebrate the years
behind us they become
stepping-stones of strength
and joy for the years ahead.

It is such a comfort to drop
the tangles of life into God's
hands and leave them there.

L. B. COWMAN

FEBRUARY 26

The Lord will accomplish what
concerns me; Your lovingkindness,
O Lord, is everlasting; Do not
forsake the works of Your hands.

PSALM 138:8 NASB

FEBRUARY 27

God has given us two hands—
one to receive with and the
other to give with. We are
not cisterns made for hoarding.
We are channels made for sharing.

BILLY GRAHAM

FEBRUARY 28

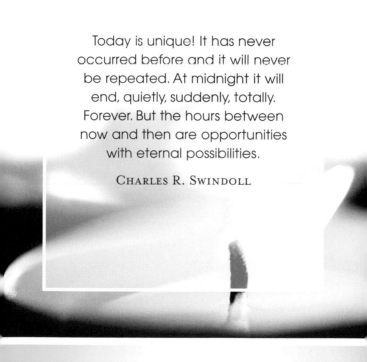

Today is unique! It has never
occurred before and it will never
be repeated. At midnight it will
end, quietly, suddenly, totally.
Forever. But the hours between
now and then are opportunities
with eternal possibilities.

CHARLES R. SWINDOLL

FEBRUARY 29

If I can keep laughing,
everything will be fine.

BEVERLY SILLS

*Satisfy us in the morning with Your
unfailing love, that we may sing
for joy and be glad all our days.*

PSALM 90:14 NIV

MARCH 1

God loves us for ourselves.
He values our love more
than He values galaxies
of new created worlds.

A. W. Tozer

Every day holds the possibility
of a miracle.

Nothing is impossible with God.

Luke 1:37 niv

March 3

Not knowing when
the dawn will come
I open every door.

EMILY DICKINSON

The great truths of God must
never be obscured or withheld
under the guise of complexity,
big words or alleged spiritual
depth.... Depth is about
believing more and more in
Jesus Christ and the truth of God.

LEITH ANDERSON

The true way of softening
one's troubles is to
solace those of others.

MADAME DE MAINTENON

MARCH 6

I know that God is at work
in the regularness of
my days. May I recognize
His hand when I see it.

GLORIA GAITHER

God is our refuge and strength,
an ever-present help in trouble.
Therefore we will not fear....
The Lord Almighty is with us.

PSALM 46:1-2,7 NIV

MARCH 8

I would sooner live in a
cottage and wonder at
everything than live in a castle
and wonder at nothing.

JOAN WINMILL BROWN

MARCH 9

Faith means you want God
and want to want nothing else....
In faith there is movement
and development.
Each day something is new.

BRENNAN MANNING

MARCH 10

Nothing is so strong
as gentleness,
and nothing so gentle
as real strength.

FRANCIS DE SALES

MARCH 11

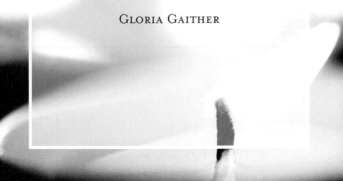

Every time I begin to feel
that there just isn't any
more strength in me,
I end up knowing that
there is more...in Him.

GLORIA GAITHER

I love the Lord because He
hears my prayers and answers
them. Because He bends
down and listens, I will
pray as long as I breathe!

Psalm 116:1-2 tlb

March 13

Begin today! No matter how feeble
the light, let it shine as best it may.
The world may need just that
quality of light which you have.

HENRY C. BLINN

MARCH 14

Oh, the comfort, the inexpressible
comfort of feeling safe
with a person: having
neither to weigh thoughts
nor measure words,
but to pour them out.

DINAH MARIA MULOCK CRAIK

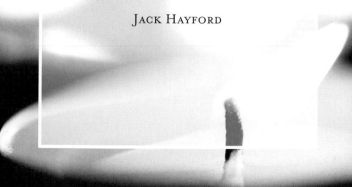

In God's wisdom, He frequently
chooses to meet our
needs by showing His love
toward us through the hands
and hearts of others.

JACK HAYFORD

MARCH 16

What value has compassion
that does not take
its object in its arms?

ANTOINE DE SAINT-EXUPERY

MARCH 17

Rejoice in the Lord always.
I will say it again: Rejoice!
Let your gentleness be
evident to all. The Lord is near.

PHILIPPIANS 4:4–5 NIV

MARCH 18

At times it is only necessary
to rest one's self in silence
for a few minutes, in order
to take off the pressure and
become wonderfully refreshed.

DRESSER

MARCH 19

Dedicate yourself to the
call of your heart and see
where it leads you.

Silences make the real
conversations between friends.
Not the saying but the never
needing to say is what counts.

MARGARET LEE RUNBECK

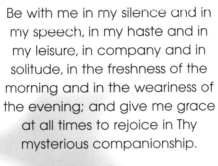

Be with me in my silence and in
my speech, in my haste and in
my leisure, in company and in
solitude, in the freshness of the
morning and in the weariness of
the evening; and give me grace
at all times to rejoice in Thy
mysterious companionship.

JOHN BAILLE

MARCH 22

Night by night I will lie down
and sleep in the thought of God.

WILLIAM MOUNTFORD

*Many, O Lord my God, are Your
wonderful works which You have
done; and Your thoughts toward
us cannot be recounted to
You in order; if I would declare
and speak of them, they are
more than can be numbered.*

PSALM 40:5 NKJV

MARCH 23

The great thing to remember
is that, though our
feelings come and go,
His love for us does not.

C.S. LEWIS

The most extraordinary thing about the oyster is this. Irritations get into his shell.... And when he cannot get rid of them, he uses the irritations to do the loveliest thing an oyster ever has the chance to do. If there are irritations in our lives today, there is only one prescription: make a pearl. It may have to be a pearl of patience, but, anyhow, make a pearl. And it takes faith and love to do it.

HARRY EMERSON FOSDICK

MARCH 25

Start by doing what's
necessary, then what's
possible and suddenly you
are doing the impossible.

FRANCIS OF ASSISI

Still round the corner
there may wait, a new road,
or a secret gate.

J. R. R. TOLKIEN

MARCH 27

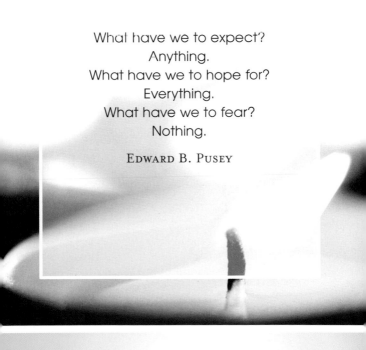

What have we to expect?
Anything.
What have we to hope for?
Everything.
What have we to fear?
Nothing.

EDWARD B. PUSEY

All God's words are right,
and everything He does
is worthy of our trust.
He loves whatever is just
and good; the earth
is filled with His tender love.

PSALM 33:4-5 TLB

MARCH 29

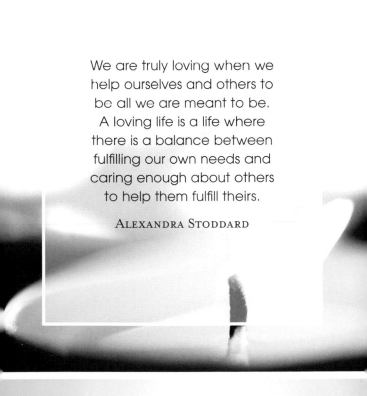

We are truly loving when we help ourselves and others to be all we are meant to be. A loving life is a life where there is a balance between fulfilling our own needs and caring enough about others to help them fulfill theirs.

ALEXANDRA STODDARD

MARCH 30

At every crossroad,
follow your dream.
It is courageous to let
your heart lead the way.

THOMAS LELAND

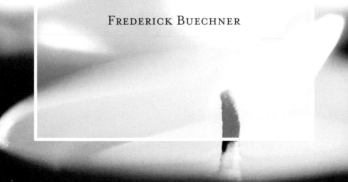

Without somehow destroying me
in the process, how could God
reveal Himself in a way that
would leave no room for doubt?
If there were no room for doubt,
there would be no room for me.

FREDERICK BUECHNER

APRIL 1

May our Lord Jesus Christ Himself and God our Father, who has loved us and given us everlasting comfort and hope, which we don't deserve, comfort your hearts with all comfort, and help you in every good thing you say and do.

2 Thessalonians 2:16-17 tlb

April 2

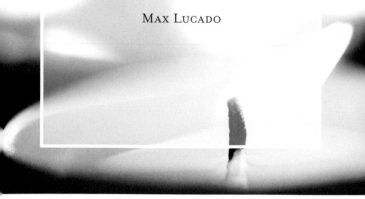

Hope is not a granted wish or a
favor performed; no, it is far greater
than that. It is a zany, unpredictable
dependence on a God who loves
to surprise us out of our socks.

Max Lucado

There are moments when our hearts nearly burst within us for the sheer joy of being alive. The first sight of our newborn babies, the warmth of love in another's eyes, the fresh scent of rain on a hot summer's eve—moments like these renew in us a heartfelt appreciation for life.

GWEN WEISING

APRIL 4

Open your hearts to the love
God instills.... God loves you
tenderly. What He gives you
is not to be kept under lock
and key, but to be shared.

MOTHER TERESA

To be glad of life, because it gives you the chance to love and to work and to play and to look up at the stars; to be satisfied with your possessions, but not contented with yourself until you have made the best of them;...to think seldom of your enemies, often of your friends, and every day of Christ; and to spend as much time as you can, with body and with spirit in God's out-of-doors—these are little guideposts on the footpath to peace.

HENRY VAN DYKE

Sometimes we just need
to slow down and grow.

Lois Wyse

*The Lord is my Shepherd....
He makes me lie down
in green pastures, He leads
me beside quiet waters,
He restores my soul.*

Psalm 23:1 niv

The ordinary acts we practice
every day at home are of more
importance to the soul than
their simplicity might suggest.

THOMAS MOORE

This is and has been the
Father's work from the
beginning—to bring us
into the home of His heart.

GEORGE MACDONALD

The goal of grace is to create
a love relationship between
God and us who believe,
the kind of relationship for
which we were first made.

J. I. PACKER

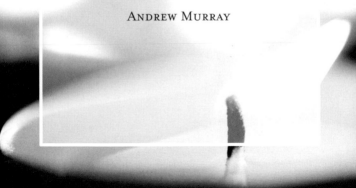

If the Lord be with us, we have no
cause to fear. His eye is upon us,
His arm over us, His ear open to
our prayer—His grace sufficient,
His promise unchangeable.

ANDREW MURRAY

APRIL 11

Do not fear, for I am with you;
do not be dismayed, for I am
your God. I will strengthen you
and help you; I will uphold you
with My righteous right hand.

ISAIAH 41:10 NIV

APRIL 12

(God) stands fast as your rock,
steadfast as your safeguard,
sleepless as your watcher,
valiant as your champion.

CHARLES H. SPURGEON

Love is not about what we do,
but who we are, convincing
others of our love for them...
and about who loves us.

JACK FROST

APRIL 14

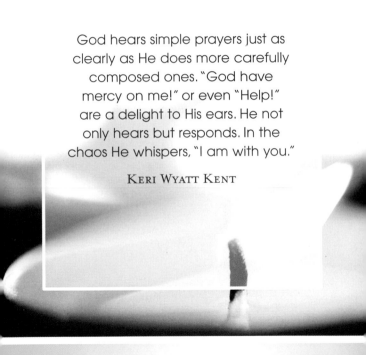

God hears simple prayers just as clearly as He does more carefully composed ones. "God have mercy on me!" or even "Help!" are a delight to His ears. He not only hears but responds. In the chaos He whispers, "I am with you."

KERI WYATT KENT

God understands our prayers
even when we can't find
the words to say them.

April 16

Since He did not spare even
His own Son for us but gave
Him up for us all, won't He also
surely give us everything else?

ROMANS 8:32 TLB

APRIL 17

The Lord's chief desire is to reveal Himself to you, in order for Him to do that He gives you abundant grace. The Lord gives you the experience of enjoying His presence. He touches you, and His touch is so delightful that, more than ever, you are drawn inwardly to Him.

MADAME JEANNE GUYON

APRIL 18

What the dew is to the flower,
gentle words are to the soul.

POLLY RUPE

*Your gentleness has
made me great.*

PSALM 18:35 TLB

I am convinced that God has
built into all of us an appreciation
of beauty and has even allowed
us to participate in the creation
of beautiful things and places.
It may be one way God brings
healing to our brokenness, and a
way that we can contribute
toward bringing wholeness to
our fallen world.

MARY JANE WORDEN

APRIL 20

His grace is great enough to meet
the great things—the crashing
waves that overwhelm the soul,
the roaring winds that leave us
stunned and breathless, the sudden
storms beyond our life's control.

ANNIE JOHNSON FLINT

There is no fear in love.
But perfect love drives out fear....
We love because he first loved us.

1 JOHN 4:18-19 NIV

APRIL 22

The world is full of suffering.
It is also full of
the overcoming of it.

HELEN KELLER

Tuck (this) thought into your
heart today. Treasure it.
Your Father God cares
about your daily everythings
that concern you.

KAY ARTHUR

A friend is one who joyfully sings
with you when you are on
the mountain top, and silently walks
beside you through the valley.

WILLIAM A WARD

APRIL 25

I am glad that in the springtime
of life there were those who
planted flowers of love in my heart.

ROBERT LOUIS STEVENSON

APRIL 26

I have thoroughly tested
Your promises and that is why
I love them so much.

Psalm 119:140 tlb

April 27

The Christian life is that our
hearts might be restored
and set free. That's the deal.
That's what Jesus came to do,
by His own announcement.
Jesus wants life for us.

JOHN ELDRIDGE

APRIL 28

A bird does not sing because
he has an answer—he sings
because he has a song.

BARBARA JOHNSON

All that we have and are is one
of the unique and never-to-be
repeated ways God has chosen
to express Himself in space and
time. Each of us, made in
His image and likeness, is yet
another promise He has made
to the universe that He will
continue to love it and care for it.

BRENNAN MANNING

Influence often isn't noticed
until it blossoms later in the
garden of someone else's life.
Our words and actions may
land close to home, or they
may be carried far and wide.

PAM FARREL

MAY 1

The possibilities of prayer
run parallel with the promises
of God. Prayer opens an
outlet for the promises...
and secures their precious ends.

E. M. BOUNDS

Hold fast your dreams!
Within your heart
Keep one still, secret spot
Where dreams may go
And, sheltered so,
May thrive and grow.

LOUISE DRISCOLL

MAY 3

The soul should always
stand ajar, ready to welcome
the ecstatic experience.

MAY 4

Let God have you, and let
God love you—and don't
be surprised if your heart
begins to hear music you've
never heard and your feet
learn to dance as never before.

MAX LUCADO

The remarkable truth is that
our choices matter, not just to
us and our own destiny but,
amazingly, to God Himself
and the universe He rules.

PHILIP YANCEY

MAY 6

Blessed be the Lord, who daily
loadeth us with benefits,
even the God of our salvation.

PSALM 68:19 KJV

MAY 7

The stars exist that we might know
how high our dreams can soar.

MAY 8

God will never, never, never let
us down if we have faith
and put our trust in Him.
He will always look after us.

MOTHER TERESA

When I look back at where
I've been, I see that what I am
becoming is a whole lot further
down the road from where I was.

GLORIA GAITHER

MAY 10

Oh Lord God,
I have no idea where I am going,
I do not see the road ahead of me,
I cannot know for certain
where it will end....
I will not fear,
for You are ever with me,
and You will never leave me.

Thomas Merton

Find rest, O my soul, in God alone;
my hope comes from Him.

PSALM 62:5 NIV

MAY 12

Lift up your eyes. The heavenly
Father waits to bless you—
in inconceivable ways to
make your life what you
never dreamed it could be.

ANNE ORTLUND

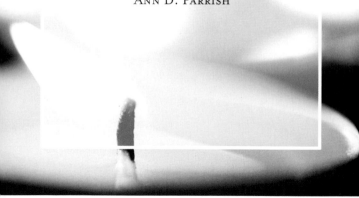

A friend understands what you are
trying to say...even when your
thoughts aren't fitting into words.

Ann D. Parrish

May 14

The fruit of our placing all things in His hands is the presence of His abiding peace in our hearts.

MAY 15

Let my soul take refuge...
beneath the shadow of
Your wings: let my heart,
this sea of restless waves,
find peace in You, O God.

AUGUSTINE

MAY 16

King David quoted Jesus as saying:
"I know the Lord is always with me.
He is helping me. God's mighty
power supports me. No wonder
my heart is filled with joy and my
tongue shouts His praises! For I know
all will be well with me in death."

ACTS 2:25-26 TLB

I have seen what a laugh
can do. It can transform almost
unbearable tears into something
bearable, even hopeful.

Bob Hope

May 18

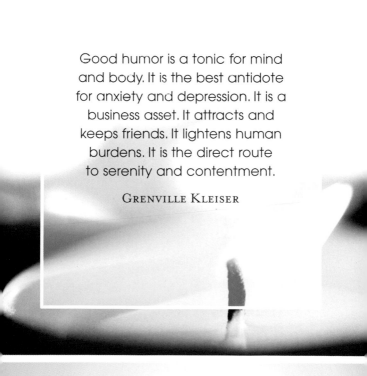

Good humor is a tonic for mind and body. It is the best antidote for anxiety and depression. It is a business asset. It attracts and keeps friends. It lightens human burdens. It is the direct route to serenity and contentment.

GRENVILLE KLEISER

What shall I bestow upon a friend?
Fleeting moments of silent blessings;
trust in tomorrow, which is life's
hardest task; faith that each new
dawn brings daylight's golden
pathway to the ever-open door;
and a belief that God will be with
them though all others go their way.

LEA PALMER

MAY 20

The grace of God...there's only
one catch. Like any other gift,
the gift of grace can be yours
only if you'll reach out and take it.
Maybe being able to reach
out and take it is a gift too.

FREDERICK BUECHNER

We can rejoice, too, when we run
into problems and trials, for we know
that they are good for us—they help
us learn to be patient. And patience
develops strength of character in
us and helps us trust God more each
time we use it until finally our hope
and faith are strong and steady.

Romans 5:3-4 tlb

May 22

God's love...is a beautiful,
eternal gift, held out to us
in the hands of love.

JOHN POWELL, S. J.

We must not, in trying to think
about how we can make a big
difference, ignore the small daily
differences we can make which,
over time, add up to big differences
that we often cannot foresee.

MARIAN WRIGHT EDELMAN

MAY 24

God has something new for
you every day. He delights
in you and loves to surprise
you with good things.

ROY LESSIN

The God who created, names,
and numbers the stars in the
heavens also numbers the
hairs of my head.... He pays
attention to very big things
and to very small ones. What
matters to me matters to Him,
and that changes my life.

ELISABETH ELLIOT

Are not five sparrows sold for two pennies? Yet not one of them is forgotten by God. Indeed, the very hairs of your head are all numbered. Don't be afraid; you are worth more than many sparrows.

LUKE 12:6-7 NIV

When you get into a tight place
and everything goes against you,
till it seems as though you could
not hang on a minute longer, never
give up then, for that is just the
place and time that the tide will turn.

HARRIET BEECHER STOWE

Time has a wonderful way of
showing us what really matters.

He has made everything
beautiful in its time.

ECCLESIASTES 3:11 NIV

Like a plant that starts up in showers and sunshine and does not know which has best helped it to grow, it is difficult to say whether the hard things or the pleasant things did me the most good.

LUCY LARCOM

MAY 30

God has a thousand ways
Where I can see not one;
When all my means have
reached their end
Then His have just begun.

ESTHER GUYOT

Happy are the kind and merciful,
for they shall be shown mercy.
Happy are those whose hearts
are pure, for they shall see God.

MATTHEW 5:7-8 TLB

JUNE 1

God's glorious grace says: "Throw guilt and anxiety overboard— draw the anchor—trim the sails— man the rudder—a strong gale of My Spirit is coming!"

CHARLES R. SWINDOLL

God's love never ceases.
Never.... Our faith does not
earn it anymore than our
stupidity jeopardizes it.
God doesn't love us less if
we fail or more if we succeed.
God's love never ceases.

MAX LUCADO

We are made to reach out
beyond our grasp.

OSWALD CHAMBERS

*I pray that you, being rooted
and established in love,
may have power... to grasp
how wide and long and high
and deep is the love of Christ.*

EPHESIANS 3:17-18 NIV

Be patient with yourself and others.
There are no shortcuts to spirituality.
Growing fruit takes time.

What God sends is better
than what we ask for.

Now to Him who is able to do
exceeding abundantly beyond all
that we ask or think, according
to the power that works within us.

EPHESIANS 3:20 NASB

We can make up our minds
whether our lives in this world
shall...be beautiful and fragrant
like the lilies of the field.

FATHER ANDREW

JUNE 7

Isn't is splendid to think of all the things there are to find out about? It just makes me feel glad to be alive—it's such an interesting world. It wouldn't be half so interesting if we knew all about everything.

LUCY MAUD MONTGOMERY

The miracle of joy is this: It happens when there is no apparent reason for it. Circumstances may call for despair. Yet something different rouses itself inside us.... We are able to remember what the sunrise looks like.... We remember God. We remember He is love. We remember He is near.

RUTH SENTER

Hope means to keep living
amid desperation and to keep
humming in the darkness.

Henri J. M. Nouwen

Now may the God of hope
fill you with all joy and
peace in believing, that you
may abound in hope by
the power of the Holy Spirit.

ROMANS 15:13 NASB

JUNE 11

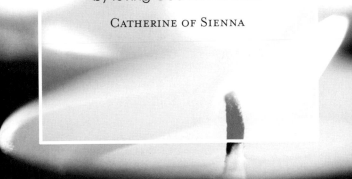

We are of such value to God
that He came to live among us...
and to guide us home.
He will go to any length to
seek us.... We can only respond
by loving God for His love.

CATHERINE OF SIENNA

At the very heart of the
universe is God's desire
to give and to forgive.

I believe that God is in me
as the sun is in the color
and fragrance of a flower—
the Light in my darkness,
the Voice in my silence.

HELEN KELLER

The work of creating is an act of love. The God who flung from His fingertips this universe filled with galaxies and stars, penguins and puffins...peaches and pears, and a world full of children made in His own image, is the God who loves with magnificent monotony.

BRENNAN MANNING

JUNE 15

He is like a father to us,
tender and sympathetic....
The lovingkindness of the Lord
is from everlasting to everlasting,
to those who reverence Him.

PSALM 103:13, 17 TLB

JUNE 16

Don't be ashamed to be as a
child in your relationship to God.
Let the everlasting arms rock
you to sleep.... He will take care
of you day and night, forever.

NORMAN VINCENT PEALE

JUNE 17

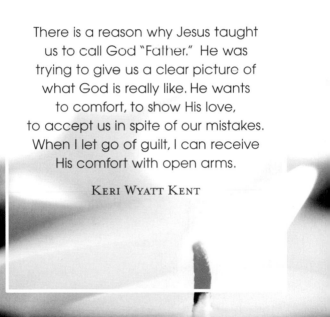

There is a reason why Jesus taught
us to call God "Father." He was
trying to give us a clear picture of
what God is really like. He wants
to comfort, to show His love,
to accept us in spite of our mistakes.
When I let go of guilt, I can receive
His comfort with open arms.

KERI WYATT KENT

Joy comes from knowing God loves me and knows who I am and where I'm going...that my future is secure as I rest in Him.

JAMES DOBSON

There is a silence into which the
world cannot intrude. There is
an ancient peace you carry
in your heart and have not lost.

I am leaving you with a gift—
peace of mind and heart!
And the peace I give isn't fragile
like the peace the world gives.
So don't be troubled or afraid.

JOHN 14:27 TLB

JUNE 21

Be still, and in the quiet moments,
listen to the voice of your
heavenly Father. His words can
renew your spirit...no one knows
you and your needs like He does.

JANET L. WEAVER

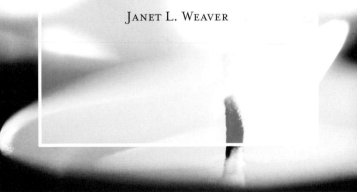

Huge waves that would frighten
an ordinary swimmer produce a
tremendous thrill for the surfer who
has ridden them.... The things
we try to avoid and fight against—
tribulation, suffering, and
persecution—are the very things
that produce abundant joy in us.

OSWALD CHAMBERS

JUNE 23

You have to have faith that there is a reason you go through certain things. I can't say I am glad to go through pain, but in a way one must, in order to gain courage and really feel joy.

CAROL BURNETT

JUNE 24

Heavenly Father,
Thank You for the opportunity
to laugh. Help me to find joy in
everything that I do. Let me laugh
and be cheerful, so that those
around me will be blessed by
my smile and my optimism. Amen.

KIM BOYCE

You have made known to me
the path of life; You will fill me with
joy in your presence, with eternal
pleasures at Your right hand.

PSALM 16:11 NIV

JUNE 26

Time, indeed, is a sacred gift,
and each day is a little life.

SIR JOHN LUBBOCK

JUNE 27

God is the friend of silence.
Trees, flowers, grass grow in silence.
See the stars, moon, and sun,
how they move in silence.

MOTHER TERESA

There is joy in heaven when
a tear of sorrow is shed in
the presence of a truly
understanding heart. And heaven
will never forget that joy.

CHARLES MALIK

JUNE 29

God, who is love—who Is, If I may
say it this way, made out of love—
simply cannot help but shed
blessing on blessing upon us.
We do not need to beg, for He
simply cannot help it!

HANNAH WHITALL SMITH

The Lord your God is with you...
He will take great delight in you,
He will quiet you with His love,
He will rejoice over you with singing.

ZEPHANIAH 3:17 NIV

JULY 1

If you can learn to laugh in spite of
the circumstances that surround you,
you will enrich others, enrich yourself,
and more than that, you will last!

BARBARA JOHNSON

JULY 2

Don't put off for tomorrow what
you can do today, because
if you enjoy it today, you can
do it again tomorrow.

JAMES MICHENER

JULY 3

God created us with an
overwhelming desire to soar....
He designed us to be tremendously
productive and "to mount
up with wings like eagles,"
realistically dreaming of what
He can do with our potential.

CAROL KENT

An infinite God can give all of
Himself to each of His children.
He does not distribute Himself that
each may have a part, but to
each one He gives all of Himself
as fully as if there were no others.

A. W. TOZER

I will rejoice in doing good to them, and I will plant them in this land in faithfulness, with all My heart and all My soul.

JEREMIAH 32:41 NRSV

I expect to pass through this life
but once. If, therefore, there be
any kindness I can show, or any
good thing I can do to any
fellow being, let me do it now,
and not deter or neglect it,
as I shall not pass this way again.

WILLIAM PENN

How quietly a rose buds,
breaks, blossoms,
bestows its blessings, falls.

PAM BROWN

Love to me is when you walk
out on that one more thing
and say, "Nothing will
come between me and one.
Not even one thing."

SARA GROVES

JULY 9

By love alone is God enjoyed;
by love alone delighted in,
by love alone approached and
admired. His nature requires love.

THOMAS TRAHERNE

Bless every humble soul who,
in these days of stress and strain,
preaches sermons without words.

PETER MARSHALL

JULY 11

Happiness turns up more or less
where you'd expect it to be—
a good marriage, a rewarding
job, a pleasant vacation.
Joy, on the other hand, is as
notoriously unpredictable as
the One who bequeaths it.

FREDERICK BUECHNER

The life we have been given
can't be bought or bargained for.
It is a gift. Every good and perfect
gift comes from above…coming
down from the Father of lights
in whom there is no variation or
shifting shadow (James 1:17).
If our day is indeed a gift from
God, something of the Giver
should be evident within the gift.

KEN GIRE

Friends remind us we are
part of something greater than
ourselves, a larger world.

BARBARA JENKINS

JULY 14

Courage is contagious.
When a brave man takes
a stand, the spines of
others are often stiffened.

BILLY GRAHAM

So let no one despise him.
But send him on his way in peace,
so that he may come to Me;
for I expect him with the brethren.

1 Corinthians 16:11 NASB

Don't think so much about who
is for or against you, rather give
all your care, that God be
with you in everything you do.

THOMAS À KEMPIS

JULY 17

Love means to love that which
is unlovable, or it is no virtue at all;
forgiving means to pardon that
which is unpardonable, or it is no
virtue at all—and to hope means
hoping when things are hopeless,
or it is no virtue at all.

G. K. CHESTERTON

There is not a heart but has
its moments of longing, yearning
for something better, nobler,
holier than it knows now.

HENRY WARD BEECHER

JULY 19

In a special way, human beings…
being made in the image of
God, only become real human
beings, are only able to grow
and thrive as human beings,
as they also yearn for God.

ROBERTA BONDI

What a wonderful God we have—
He is...the source of every mercy,
and the one who so wonderfully
comforts and strengthens us.

2 Corinthians 1:3-4 TLB

July 21

Memories, important yesterdays,
were once todays.
Treasure and notice today.

Gloria Gaither

July 22

That is God's call to us—simply
to be people who are content
to live close to Him and to renew
the kind of life in which the
closeness is felt and experienced.

THOMAS MERTON

Faith has to be exercised
in the midst of ordinary,
down-to-earth living.

ELISABETH ELLIOT

I know that God is faithful.
I know that He answers
prayers, many times in ways
I may not understand.

SHEILA WALSH

JULY 25

As far as God is concerned,
there is a sweet, wholesome
fragrance in our lives. It is the
fragrance of Christ within us.

2 Corinthians 2:15 tlb

July 26

True silence is the rest of
the mind; it is to the spirit
what sleep is to the body,
nourishment and refreshment.

WILLIAM PENN

He is right here. With an unyielding
desire that is willing to trust,
we may call out to our heavenly
Father and know that He will
answer, filling our hearts with
bright joy and freshness of life.

Friends are an indispensable part of a meaningful life. They are the ones who share our burdens and multiply our blessings. A true friend sticks by us in our joys and sorrows. In good times and bad, we need friends who will pray for us, listen to us, and lend a comforting hand.

BEVERLY LaHAYE

JULY 29

The God who created the
vast resources of the universe
is also the inventor of the
human mind. His inspired
words of encouragement
guarantee us that we can live
above our circumstances.

JAMES DOBSON

Therefore, as God's chosen
people, holy and dearly loved,
clothe yourselves with
compassion, kindness, humility,
gentleness and patience.

COLOSSIANS 3:12 NIV

JULY 31

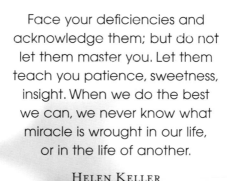

Face your deficiencies and acknowledge them; but do not let them master you. Let them teach you patience, sweetness, insight. When we do the best we can, we never know what miracle is wrought in our life, or in the life of another.

HELEN KELLER

Indeed, we do not really live
unless we have friends
surrounding us like a firm wall
against the winds of the world.

CHARLES HANSON TOWNE

AUGUST 2

Always begin anew with
the day, just as nature does;
it is one of the sensible things
that nature does.

GEORGE E. WOODBURY

We may...depend upon God's
promises, for...He will be as good
as His word. He is so kind that
He cannot deceive us, so true
that He cannot break His promise.

MATTHEW HENRY

AUGUST 4

Forever, O Lord, Your Word stands
firm in heaven. Your faithfulness
extends to every generation,
like the earth You created;
it endures by Your decree,
for everything serves Your plans.

PSALM 119:89-90 TLB

AUGUST 5

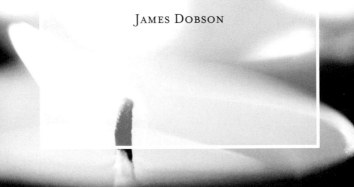

The Lord doesn't always remove
the sources of stress in our lives...
but He's always there and
cares for us. We can feel His arms
around us on the darkest night.

JAMES DOBSON

AUGUST 6

Prayer is not asking. Prayer is putting oneself in the hands of God, at His disposition, and listening to His voice in the depths or our hearts.

Mother Teresa

Rest is not idleness, and to lie
sometimes on the grass under
the trees on a summer's day,
listening to the murmur of water,
or watching the clouds
float across the sky, is by no
means a waste of time.

JOHN LUBBOCK

AUGUST 8

Time Is a very precious gift of God;
so precious that it's only given
to us moment by moment.

AMELIA BARR

AUGUST 9

He Himself gives life and
breath to everything and
satisfies every need there is.

ACTS 17:25 TLB

AUGUST 10

You can come out of the furnace
of trouble two ways: if you let it
consume you, you come out
a cinder; but there is a kind of
metal which refuses to be
consumed, and comes out a star.

JEAN CHURCH

Delicate threads of hope,
patiently woven, become
the strong fabric of our faith.

Janet L. Weaver Smith

August 12

Perhaps this moment is unclear, but let it be—even if the next, and many moments after that are unclear, let them be. Trust that God will help you work them out, and that all the unclear moments will bring you to that moment of clarity and action when you are known by Him and know Him. These are the better and brighter moments of His blessing.

Dare to love and to be a real friend. The love you give and receive is a reality that will lead you closer and closer to God as well as to those whom God has given you to love.

HENRI J. M. NOUWEN

AUGUST 14

May the Lord continually bless
you with heaven's blessings
as well as with human joys.

PSALM 128:5 TLB

AUGUST 15

For all of us, whether we walk
old paths or blaze new trails,
friends remain important.

Lois Wyse

August 16

There is nourishment from
being encouraged and held
up by others when we are weak.
We are nourished from feedback
from friends whom we trust
and who will be honest with us.

RICH G. BUHLER

It is not what we do that matters,
but what a sovereign God chooses
to do through us. God doesn't
want our success; He wants us.

CHARLES COLSON

Moments spent listening,
talking, playing, and sharing
together may be the most
important times of all.

GLORIA GAITHER

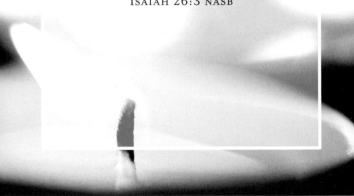

The steadfast of mind You
will keep in perfect peace,
because he trusts in You.

Isaiah 26:3 nasb

August 20

Each one of us is God's special
work of art. Through us, He
teaches and inspires, delights
and encourages, informs and
uplifts all those who view our lives.

Joni Eareckson Tada

In the deepest heart of every man,
God planted a longing for Himself,
as He is: a God of love.

EUGENIA PRICE

AUGUST 22

We walk without fear, full of hope
and courage and strength to do
His will, waiting for the endless good
which He is always giving as fast as
He can get us able to take it in.

GEORGE MACDONALD

For whatever life holds for you
and your family in the coming
days, weave the unfailing fabric
of God's Word through your heart
and mind. It will hold strong,
even if the rest of life unravels.

GIGI GRAHAM TCHIVIDJIAN

In quietness and trust is your strength.... The Lord longs to be gracious to you; He rises to show you compassion.

ISAIAH 30:15, 18 NIV

AUGUST 25

Eating lunch with a friend. Trying to do a decent day's work. Hearing the rain patter against the window. There is no event so commonplace but that God is present within it, always hiddenly, always leaving you room to recognize Him or not recognize Him, but all the more fascinatingly because of that, all the more compellingly and hauntingly.

FREDERICK BUECHNER

AUGUST 26

You have a unique message to
deliver, a unique song to sing,
a unique act of love to bestow.
This message, this song, and this
act of love have been entrusted
exclusively to the one and only you.

JOHN POWELL, S. J.

If you are seeking after God,
you may be sure of this: God is
seeking you much more. He is the
Lover, and you are His beloved.
He has promised Himself to you.

JOHN OF THE CROSS

AUGUST 28

Heavenly Father,
Teach me not to procrastinate
but to do what I can today,
because there is no promise of
tomorrow. Lead me to those people
who are in need of something
that I can give. I want to be
available for You to use in any way
that You should choose. Amen.

KIM BOYCE

He is good to everyone, and
His compassion is intertwined
with everything He does.

Psalm 145:9 tlb

August 30

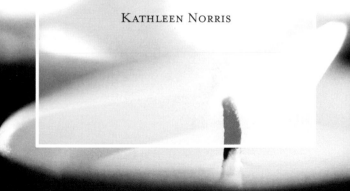

None of us knows what the next
change is going to be, what
unexpected opportunity is just
around the corner, waiting to
change all the tenor of our lives.

KATHLEEN NORRIS

AUGUST 31

Times of solitude help keep my
focus on God during times
when I am surrounded and
overwhelmed by the cares and
commitments of my life.

KERI WYATT KENT

SEPTEMBER 1

You can trust God right now
to supply all your needs
for today. And if your needs
are more tomorrow, His supply
will be greater also.

SEPTEMBER 2

It is not the work we do that is
so important. It's the people
we work with. It's the work God
does in our lives through them.
And it's the work He does in their
lives through us. That is what's
sacred. Slowing down and stopping
is our way of acknowledging it.

KEN GIRE

SEPTEMBER 3

Yes, the gladness You have given me is far greater than their joys at harvest time as they gaze at their bountiful crops. I will lie down in peace and sleep, for though I am alone, O Lord, You will keep me safe.

PSALM 4:7-8 TLB

SEPTEMBER 4

When you have laboriously
accomplished your daily task,
go to sleep in peace.
God is awake.

Victor Hugo

God is never in a hurry but spends years with those He expects to greatly use. He never thinks the days of preparation too long or too dull.

MRS. CHARLES E. COWMAN

God is every moment totally
aware of each one of us.
Totally aware in intense
concentration and love.

EUGENIA PRICE

SEPTEMBER 7

The soul would have no rainbow
had the eye no tear.

SEPTEMBER 8

Blessed is the Lord, for He has shown
me that His never-failing love
protects me like the walls of a fort!

PSALM 31:21 TLB

SEPTEMBER 9

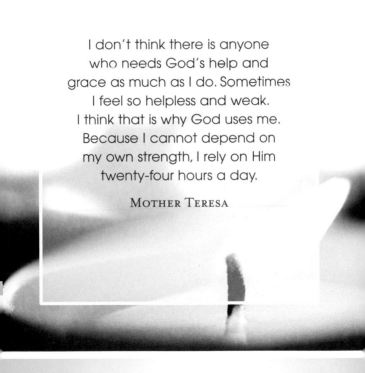

I don't think there is anyone
who needs God's help and
grace as much as I do. Sometimes
I feel so helpless and weak.
I think that is why God uses me.
Because I cannot depend on
my own strength, I rely on Him
twenty-four hours a day.

MOTHER TERESA

SEPTEMBER 10

Love is a fabric which never
fades, no matter how often
it is washed in the waters
of adversity and grief.

It's usually through our hard times, the unexpected and not-according-to-plan times, that we experience God in more intimate ways. We discover an unquenchable longing to know Him more. It's a passion that isn't concerned that life fall within certain predictable lines, but a passion that pursues God and knows He is relentless in His pursuit of each one of us.

SEPTEMBER 12

My friends have made the story
of my life. In a thousand ways,
they have turned my limitations
into beautiful privileges,
and enabled me to walk
serene and happy in the
shadow cast by my deprivation.

HELEN KELLER

SEPTEMBER 13

In response to all He has done
for us, let us outdo each other
in being helpful and kind to
each other and in doing good.

HEBREWS 10:24 TLB

SEPTEMBER 14

Sometimes it is a slender thread,
Sometimes a strong, stout rope;
She clings to one end,
I the other;
She calls it friendship;
I call it hope.

Lois Wyse

September 15

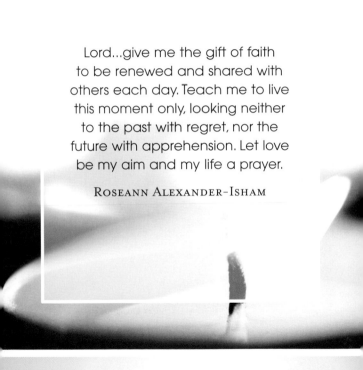

Lord...give me the gift of faith
to be renewed and shared with
others each day. Teach me to live
this moment only, looking neither
to the past with regret, nor the
future with apprehension. Let love
be my aim and my life a prayer.

ROSEANN ALEXANDER-ISHAM

SEPTEMBER 16

There will come a time when
you believe everything is finished.
That will be the beginning.

LOUIS L'AMOUR

SEPTEMBER 17

If it can be verified, we don't need faith.... Faith is for that which lies on the other side of reason. Faith is what makes life bearable, with all its tragedies and ambiguities and sudden, startling joys.

MADELEINE L'ENGLE

If you want to know what God wants you to do, ask Him, and He will gladly tell you, for He is always ready to give a bountiful supply of wisdom to all who ask Him; He will not resent it. But when you ask Him, be sure that you really expect Him to tell you, for a doubtful mind will be as unsettled as a wave of the sea that is driven and tossed by the wind.

JAMES 1:5-6 TLB

SEPTEMBER 19

May God give you eyes
to see beauty only
the heart can understand.

SEPTEMBER 20

Courage...is when you know
you're licked before you begin
but you begin anyway and you
see it through no matter what.

HARPER LEE

SEPTEMBER 21

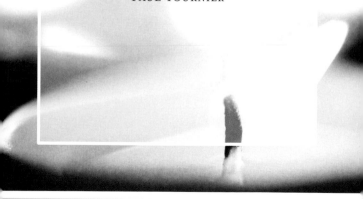

It is impossible to overemphasize
the immense need men
have to be really listened to.

PAUL TOURNIER

SEPTEMBER 22

Notice words of compassion.
Seek out deeds of kindness.
These are like the doves from
heaven, pointing out to you
who are the ones blessed with
inner grace and beauty.

CHRISTOPHER DE VINCK

SEPTEMBER 23

Timely advice is as lovely as
gold apples in a silver basket.

Proverbs 25:11 TLB

September 24

God created us as human
beings with the need for intimacy,
to know and be known.
And His perfect plan is to provide
us with a beautiful way to
meet that need: fellowship with
Him and with each other.

JACK FROST

All the absurd little meetings,
decisions, and skirmishes that
go to make up our days. It all
adds up to very little, and yet
it all adds up to very much.
Our days are full of nonsense,
and yet not, because it is
precisely into the nonsense of
our days that God speaks to
us words of great significance.

FREDERICK BUECHNER

Spirituality is not one compartment
or sphere of life. Rather, it is
a lifestyle: the process of life
lived with the vision of faith.

BRENNAN MANNING

Embrace your uniqueness.
Time is much too short to
be living someone else's life.

KOBI YAMADA

Take delight in the Lord,
and He will give you the
desires of your heart.

Psalm 37:4 nrsv

September 29

God can do wonders with
a broken heart if you
give Him all the pieces.

VICTOR ALFSEN

Simplicity is completely absorbed
in listening to what it hears.

THOMAS MERTON

*Listen...be wise, and keep
your heart on the right path.*

PROVERBS 23:19 NIV

OCTOBER 1

Part of our job is simply to be…
always attentive to what we
are doing and what is going on
inside us, at the same time we
listen and pay attention to the
people and events around us.
Part of our job is to expect that,
if we are attentive and willing,
God will "give us prayer," will give
us the things we need, "our daily
bread," to heal and grow in love.

ROBERTA BONDI

One of the most important
responsibilities in the Christian
life is to care about others,
smile at them, and be
a friend to the friendless.

JAMES DOBSON

OCTOBER 3

True prayer is simply a quiet, sincere, genuine conversation with God. It is a two-way dialogue between friends.

W. Phillip Keller

I no longer call you servants, because a servant does not know his master's business. Instead, I have called you friends, for everything that I learned from my Father I have made known to you.

John 15:15 niv

October 4

The things which are seen are temporal, but the things which are not seen are eternal.

OCTOBER 5

Let stars stand for those things
which are ideal and radiant in life;
if we seek sincerely and strive
hard enough, it is not impossible
to reach them, even though the
goals seem distant at the onset.
And how often do we touch
stars when we find them close
by in the shining lives of great
souls, in the sparkling universe
of humanity around us!

ESTHER BALDWIN YORK

OCTOBER 6

I want to help you to grow as
beautiful as God meant you to
be when He thought of you first.

GEORGE MacDONALD

OCTOBER 7

Grace comes free of charge to
people who do not deserve it,
and I am one of those people....
Now I am trying in my own small
way to pipe the tune of grace.
I do so because I know, more
surely than I know anything, that
any pang of healing or forgiveness
or goodness I have ever felt comes
solely from the grace of God.

PHILIP YANCEY

OCTOBER 8

You have made known to me
the paths of life; You will fill me
with joy in Your presence.

ACTS 2:28 NIV

OCTOBER 9

(God) is looking for people
who will come in simple
dependence upon His grace,
and rest in simple faith upon
His greatness. At this very
moment, He's looking at you.

JACK HAYFORD

Some emotions don't make
a lot of noise. It's hard to
hear pride. Caring is real faint-
like a heartbeat. And pure love-
why, some days it's so quiet,
you don't even know it's there.

ERMA BOMBECK

OCTOBER 11

Let us believe that God is
in all our simple deeds
and learn to find Him there.

A. W. TOZER

You already know that God is
everywhere…. And where God is,
there is heaven—heaven!
where His Majesty reigns in glory.

THERESA OF AVILA
(PARAPHRASED BY DAVID HAZARD)

OCTOBER 13

God's peace...is far more
wonderful than the human
mind can understand.
His peace will keep your
thoughts and your hearts
quiet and at rest as you
trust in Christ Jesus.

PHILIPPIANS 4:7 TLB

OCTOBER 14

You are valuable just because
you exist. Not because of what
you do or what you have done,
but simply because you are.

MAX LUCADO

It is the simple truth that holds
you together in the most complex
situations. Not simplistic, but simple.
The profound truth that the Bible
gives us is like a warm blanket
wrapped around us on a cold night.

CHARLES R. SWINDOLL

Snuggle in God's arms.
When you are hurting, when you
feel lonely...let Him cradle you,
comfort you, reassure you of His
all-sufficient power and love.

Kay Arthur

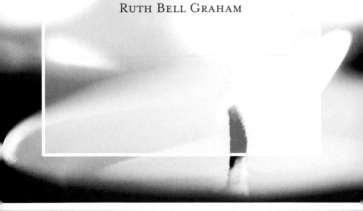

When we are away from God,
He misses us far more
than we miss Him.

RUTH BELL GRAHAM

OCTOBER 18

While he was still a long distance away, his father saw him coming, and was filled with loving pity and ran and embraced him and kissed him.

LUKE 15:20-24 TLB

OCTOBER 19

The very possibility of friendship
with God transfigures life.
This conviction...tends inevitably
to deepen every human friendship,
to make it vastly more significant.

HENRY CHURCHILL KING

Let the day suffice, with all its joys and failings, its little triumphs and defeats. I'd happily, if sleepily, welcome evening as a time of rest, and let it slip away, losing nothing.

KATHLEEN NORRIS

OCTOBER 21

Faith in God gives Christians
the absolute confidence
that He is working for good in
our lives even when all the
evidence and emotions point
to what is bad in our lives.

LEITH ANDERSON

All joy reminds. It is never a
possession, always a desire for
something longer ago or further
away or still "about to be."

C. S. Lewis

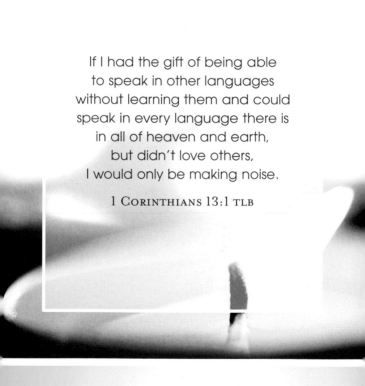

If I had the gift of being able
to speak in other languages
without learning them and could
speak in every language there is
in all of heaven and earth,
but didn't love others,
I would only be making noise.

1 Corinthians 13:1 TLB

October 24

If you think well of others,
you will also speak well of
others and to others. From the
abundance of the heart,
the mouth speaks. If your heart is
full of love, you will speak of love.

MOTHER TERESA

OCTOBER 25

Take a moment to consider the awesome reality that the God who spoke and created the universe is now speaking to you. If Jesus could speak and raise the dead, calm a storm... and heal the incurable, then what effect might a word from Him have upon your life?

HENRY T. BLACKABY

God will never let you be
shaken or moved from your
place near His heart.

JONI EARECKSON TADA

OCTOBER 27

Optimism is the faith that leads to
achievement. Nothing can be done
without hope and confidence.

HELEN KELLER

OCTOBER 28

For You are my hope, O Lord God;
You are my trust from my youth.
By You I have been upheld
from birth; You are He who took
me out of my mother's womb.
My praise shall be continually of You.

PSALM 71:5-6 NKJV

OCTOBER 29

God wants us to be present
where we are. He invites us to
see and to hear what is around
us and, through it all, to discern
the footprints of the Holy.

RICHARD J. FOSTER

Expect the dawn of a
new beginning in the
dark nights of life.

Lloyd Ogilvie

October 31

A living, loving God can and does make His presence felt, can and does speak to us in the silence of our hearts, can and does warm and caress us till we no longer doubt that He is near, that He is here.

Brennan Manning

November 1

There is an activity of the spirit, silent, unseen, which must be the dynamic of any form of truly creative, fruitful trust. When we commit a predicament, a possibility, a person to God in genuine confidence, we do not merely step aside and tap our foot until God comes through. We remain involved. We remain in contact with God in gratitude and praise. But we do this without anxiety, without worry.

EUGENIA PRICE

NOVEMBER 2

Praise be to God, who has
not rejected my prayer or
withheld His love from me!

PSALM 66:20 NIV

NOVEMBER 3

Grace tells us that we are accepted just as we are. We may not be the kind of people we want to be, we may be a long way from our goals, we may have more failures than achievements, we may not be wealthy or powerful or spiritual, we may not even be happy, but we are nonetheless accepted by God, held in His hands.

McCullough

November 4

I am not afraid of storms for I am
learning how to sail my ship.

L‍ouisa M‍ay A‍lcott

A candle loses nothing
of its light by
lighting another candle.

NOVEMBER 6

Heavenly Father,
my prayer is that I would learn
to trust You more. It's such a
comfort to know that my life
is in Your hands, and the
circumstances surrounding me
are in Your control. Remind me
daily that choosing to be happy
is an option. May I find my
strength in Your joy. Amen.

KIM BOYCE

Faith is taking the first step
even when you don't see
the whole staircase.

MARTIN LUTHER KING JR.

*Now faith is being sure of
what we hope for and certain
of what we do not see.*

HEBREWS 11:1 NIV

NOVEMBER 8

Gratitude…is not something we do at all. Rather, it is a medium of grace, a gift of God that softens the heart and enables it to see and hear and receive the things that come to it from God.

ROBERTA BONDI

Use what talents you possess:
the woods would be very
silent if no birds sang there
except those that sang best.

HENRY VAN DYKE

NOVEMBER 10

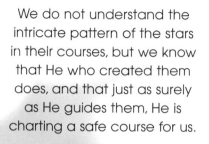

We do not understand the
intricate pattern of the stars
in their courses, but we know
that He who created them
does, and that just as surely
as He guides them, He is
charting a safe course for us.

BILLY GRAHAM

NOVEMBER 11

No man is an iceberg drifting
on the ocean of history.
Each one of us belongs to a great
family, in which he has his own
place and his own role to play.

Pope John Paul II

November 12

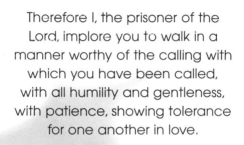

Therefore I, the prisoner of the Lord, implore you to walk in a manner worthy of the calling with which you have been called, with all humility and gentleness, with patience, showing tolerance for one another in love.

EPHESIANS 4:1-2 NASB

NOVEMBER 13

If the world seems cold to you,
Kindle fires to warm it!

MATHILDA GAGE

NOVEMBER 14

We think God's love rises and
falls with our performance.
It doesn't.... He loves you for
whose you are: you are His child.

<small>MAX LUCADO</small>

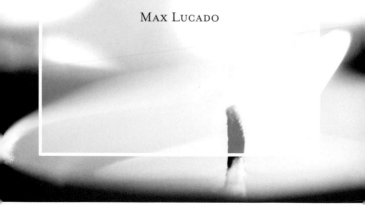

Grace and gratitude belong together like heaven and earth. Grace evokes gratitude like the voice an echo. Gratitude follows grace as thunder follows lightning.

KARL BARTH

We give thanks for the darkness of the night where lies the world of dreams…. Give us good dreams and memory of them so that we may carry their poetry and mystery into our daily lives…. Let us restore the night and reclaim it as a sanctuary of peace, where silence shall be music to our hearts and darkness shall throw light upon our souls.

MICHAEL LEUING

NOVEMBER 17

The Lord will guide you always;
He will satisfy your needs in a
sun-scorched land.... You will be
like a well-watered garden, like a
spring whose waters never fail.

ISAIAH 58:11 NIV

NOVEMBER 18

To be grateful is to recognize
the love of God in everything
He has given us—and He has
given us everything. Every breath
we draw is a gift of His love,
every moment of existence is a
gift of grace, for it brings with it
immense graces from Him.

THOMAS MERTON

Look deep within yourself and recognize what brings life and grace into your heart. It is this that can be shared with those around you. You are loved by God. This is an inspiration to love.

CHRISTOPHER DE VINCK

There is not enough darkness in
all the world to put out the light
of one small candle...any reminder
of something deeply felt or dearly
loved. No (one) is so poor as not
to have many of these small
candles. When they are lighted,
darkness goes away and
a touch of wonder remains.

ARTHUR GORDON

NOVEMBER 21

Being grateful for what we have
today doesn't mean we have to
have that forever. It means we
acknowledge that what we have
today is what we're supposed to
have today. There is enough....
And all we need will come to us.

MELODY BEATTIE

For you make me glad by
your deeds, O Lord; I sing for joy
at the works of Your hands.

PSALM 92:4 NIV

NOVEMBER 23

Live one day at a time. You've heard it before: Don't contaminate today by corrupting it with tomorrow's troubles.... Today is challenge enough! And since you will need fresh energy and new insight to handle what tomorrow throws at you, wait until it dawns before taking it on. Some of the things you do today may seem totally insignificant so far as tomorrow is concerned, but stay at it.

CHARLES R. SWINDOLL

NOVEMBER 24

Blessed are the flexible,
for they shall not be
bent out of shape.

BARBARA JOHNSON

Only God gives true peace—
a quiet gift He sets within us
just when we think we've
exhausted our search for it.

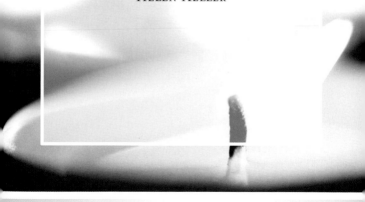

I thank God for my handicaps,
for, through them, I have found
myself, my work, and my God.

HELEN KELLER

NOVEMBER 27

Love knows no limit to its
endurance, no end to its trust,
no fading of its hope; it can
outlast anything. Love never fails.

1 Corinthians 13:7-8 Phillips

November 28

If we just give God the little
that we have, we can trust
Him to make it go around.

GLORIA GAITHER

With God there is always more
unfolding, that what we can
glimpse of the divine is always
exactly enough, and never enough.

KATHLEEN NORRIS

NOVEMBER 30

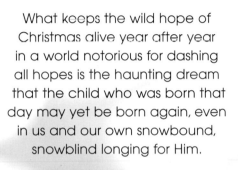

What keeps the wild hope of
Christmas alive year after year
in a world notorious for dashing
all hopes is the haunting dream
that the child who was born that
day may yet be born again, even
in us and our own snowbound,
snowblind longing for Him.

FREDERICK BUECHNER

DECEMBER 1

The uncertainties of the present
always give way to the enchanted
possibilities of the future.

GELSEY KIRKLAND

DECEMBER 2

Every good and perfect gift
is from above, coming down
from the Father of the heavenly
lights, who does not change
like shifting shadows.

JAMES 1:17 NIV

DECEMBER 3

From the heart of God comes
the strongest rhythm—the rhythm
of love. Without His love
reverberating in us, whatever we
do will come across like a noisy
gong or a clanging symbol.
And so the work of the
human heart, it seems to me,
is to listen for that music
and pick up on its rhythms.

KEN GIRE

DECEMBER 4

If instead of a gem, or even
a flower, we should cast the gift
of a loving thought into the
heart of a friend, that would
be giving as the angels give.

GEORGE MACDONALD

*Give generously, for your gifts
will return to you later.*

ECCLESIASTES 11:1 TLB

DECEMBER 5

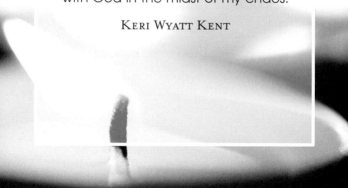

Time alone with God can help us grow, but so can serving others. Instead of feeling guilty about how little time alone I get, I need to look at how I can connect with God in the midst of my chaos.

KERI WYATT KENT

DECEMBER 6

The secret of life is that all
we have and are is a gift
of grace to be shared.

LLOYD JOHN OGILVIE

DECEMBER 7

Are you aware that the Father takes delight in you and that He thinks about you all the time?

JACK FROST

How precious also are Thy thoughts unto me, O God! how great is the sum of them! If I should count them, they are more in number than the sand: when I awake, I am still with Thee.

PSALM 139:17-18 KJV

DECEMBER 8

We encounter God in the
ordinariness of life, not in the
search for spiritual highs and
extraordinary, mystical experiences,
but in our simple presence in life.

BRENNAN MANNING

DECEMBER 9

This is the irrational season
When love blossoms bright and wild.
Had Mary been filled with reason
There'd have been no room
for the child.

MADELEINE L'ENGLE

God guides us, despite our uncertainties and our vagueness, even through our failings and mistakes.... He leads us step by step, from event to event. Only afterwards, as we look back over the way we have come and reconsider certain important moments in our lives in the light of all that has followed them...do we experience the feeling of having been led without knowing it, the feeling that God has mysteriously guided us.

PAUL TOURNIER

DECEMBER 11

God's care for us is more watchful
and more tender than the care of
any human father could possibly be.

HANNAH WHITALL SMITH

DECEMBER 12

I call on You, O God, for You will
answer me; give ear to me and
hear my prayer. Show the wonder
of Your great love…. Keep me as
the apple of Your eye; hide me
in the shadow of Your wings.

PSALM 17:6-8 NIV

DECEMBER 13

God's heart is the most sensitive
and tender of all. No act
goes unnoticed, no matter
how insignificant or small.

RICHARD J. FOSTER

DECEMBER 14

The coming of Jesus at
Bethlehem brought joy to the
world and to every human heart.
May His coming this Christmas
bring to each one of us that peace
and joy that He desires to give.

Mother Teresa

We expect too much at Christmas.
It's got to be magical.
It's got to go right. Feasting. Fun.
The perfect present. All that
anticipation. Take it easy.
Love's the thing. The rest is tinsel.

PAM BROWN

DECEMBER 16

Had my house been filled
at Bethlehem,
What should I have done
With that request
Of two for rest?
Would I have guessed
The Prince of Peace was come?

ALLISON C. WOOD

Suddenly there was with the angel a multitude of the heavenly host praising God, and saying, Glory to God in the highest, and on earth peace, good will toward men.

LUKE 2:13-14 KJV

DECEMBER 18

One taper lights a thousand,
Yet shines as it has shone;
And the humblest light may kindle
A brighter than its own.

HEZEKIAN BUTTERWORTH

DECEMBER 19

Every single act of love
bears the imprint of God.

*My beloved friends, let us continue
to love each other since love
comes from God. Everyone who
loves is born of God and
experiences a relationship with God.*

1 JOHN 4:7 THE MESSAGE

DECEMBER 20

Peace with God brings the peace
of God. It is a peace that settles
our nerves, fills our mind, floods
our spirit, and in the midst of the
uproar around us, gives us the
assurance that everything is all right.

BOB MUMFORD

Life varies its stories. Time changes everything, yet what is truly valuable—what is worth keeping— is beyond time.

RUTH SENTER

The Word became flesh and made
His dwelling among us. We have
seen His glory, the glory of the
One and Only, who came from
the Father, full of grace and truth.

JOHN 1:14 NIV

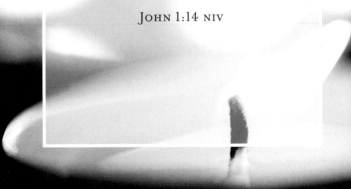

DECEMBER 23

Christmas, my child, is love in action....
When you love someone, you
give to them, as God gives to us.
The greatest gift He ever gave
was the person of His Son, sent to
us in human form so that we
might know what God the Father
is really like! Every time we love,
every time we give, it's Christmas.

DALE EVANS ROGERS

DECEMBER 24

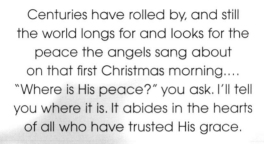

Centuries have rolled by, and still
the world longs for and looks for the
peace the angels sang about
on that first Christmas morning....
"Where is His peace?" you ask. I'll tell
you where it is. It abides in the hearts
of all who have trusted His grace.

BILLY GRAHAM

Do you believe that God is near?
He wants you to. He wants you
to know that He is in the midst
of your world. Wherever you are
as you read these words, He is
present. In your car. On the plane.
In your office, your bedroom,
your den. He's near. And He is
more than near. He is active.

MAX LUCADO

DECEMBER 26

You can never change the past.
But by the grace of God, you can
win the future. So remember
those things which will help you
forward, but forget those things
which will only hold you back.

RICHARD C. WOODSOME

DECEMBER 27

I am still confident of this:
I will see the goodness of the
Lord in the land of the living.
Wait for the Lord; be strong and
take heart and wait for the Lord.

Psalm 27:13-14 niv

December 28

We have been in God's
thought from all eternity,
and in His creative love,
His attention never leaves us.

MICHAEL QUOIST

DECEMBER 29

Whenever we realize we have not taken advantage of a magnificent opportunity, we are apt to sink into despair. Let the past sleep, but let it sleep in the sweet embrace of Christ, and let us go on into the invincible future with Him. Never let the sense of past failure defeat your next step.

OSWALD CHAMBERS

DECEMBER 30

The grace of God means
something like: Here is your life.
You might never have been,
but you are because the party
wouldn't have been complete
without you. Here is the world.
Beautiful and terrible things
will happen. Don't be afraid.
I am with you. Nothing can
ever separate us. It's for you I
created the universe. I love you.

FREDERICK BUECHNER

DECEMBER 31